@RosenTeenTalk

DISCARD
STDs AND STIs

Danielle Haynes

ROSEN
PUBLISHING

NEW YORK

Published in 2021 by The Rosen Publishing Group, Inc.
29 East 21st Street, New York, NY 10010

First Edition

Editor:Theresa Emminizer
Designer: Michael Flynn
Interior Layout: Rachel Rising

Photo Credits: Cover, pp. 1, 3, 5, 45 Alexander Raths/Shutterstock.com; cover Cosmic_Design/Shutterstock.com; cover, pp. 1, 6, 8, 10, 12, 14, 16, 18, 20, 24, 26, 28, 30, 32, 36, 38, 42 Vitya_M/Shutterstock.com; pp. 3, 13 Tony Anderson/Stone/Getty Images; pp. 3, 17 Maskot/Getty Images; pp. 3, 39 Creativa Images/Shutterstock.com; p. 6 Komsan Loonprom/Shutterstock.com; p. 7 ileezhun/Shutterstock.com; p. 9 Prostock-studio/Shutterstock.com; p. 10 Lucy Lambriex/DigitalVision/Getty Images; p. 11 Mikhail Tchkheidze/Shutterstock.com; p. 11 Wasin Borisut/Shutterstock.com; p. 12 WhiteJack/Shutterstock.com; p. 14 Lemon Tree Images/Shutterstock.com; p. 15 Volodymyr Krasyuk/Shutterstock.com; p. 18 Kateryna Kon/Shutterstock.com; p. 19 baona/E+/Getty Images; pp. 20, 26, 30 Tatiana Shepeleva/Shutterstock.com; p. 21 Tobias Arhelger/Shutterstock.com; p. 23 BSIP/Getty Images; p. 24 KATERYNA KON/SCIENCE PHOTO LIBRARY/Science Photo Library/Getty Images; p. 25 Simikov/Shutterstock.com; p. 27 Wasan Tita/Shutterstock.com; p. 28 3Dme Creative Studio/Shutterstock.com; p. 29 Cherries/Shutterstock.com; p. 32 SEBASTIAN KAULITZKI/Science Photo Library/Getty Images; p. 33 leezsnow/E+/Getty Images; p. 35 Golden Pixels LLC/Shutterstock.com; p. 36 Oleg Golovnev/Shutterstock.com; p. 37 Brasil Creativo/Shutterstock.com; p. 41 wavebreakmedia/Shutterstock.com; p. 42 John Burke/Stockbyte/Getty Images; p. 43 oneinchpunch/Shutterstock.com.

Some of the images in this book illustrate individuals who are models. The depictions do not imply actual situations or events.

Library of Congress Cataloging-in-Publication Data

Names: Haynes, Danielle, author.
Title: STDs and STIs / Danielle Haynes.
Description: New York : Rosen Publishing, [2021] I Series: @RosenTeenTalk I
  Includes index.
Identifiers: LCCN 2020007329 I ISBN 9781499468229 (library binding) I ISBN
  9781499468212 (paperback)
Subjects: LCSH: Sexually transmitted diseases—Juvenile literature.
Classification: LCC RC200.25 .H39 2021 I DDC 616.95/1dc23
LC record available at https://lccn.loc.gov/2020007329

Manufactured in the United States of America

CPSIA Compliance Information: Batch #BSR20. For further information contact Rosen Publishing, New York, New York at 1-800-237-9932.

Find us on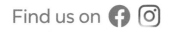

CONTENTS

Chapter 1

Feeling Unwell

I haven't been feeling great lately. A few weeks ago, I noticed it burned a little bit when I peed. There was also a little pain and swelling in my testicles.

I knew I needed to see a doctor, but I was scared. I was afraid to tell my parents. And I definitely didn't want to take off my pants in front of a doctor!

Finally, the pain got to be too much. I took the bus to a local health clinic. The doctor looked at me and did a couple tests.

A few days later, she called me back to the clinic and told me I had a sexually transmitted disease called chlamydia.

David had learned about STDs in health class, but he didn't think he could get one. He'd only had sex with one person!

WHAT IS AN STD?

You've likely heard the term "STD." Those letters stand for "sexually transmitted disease." They're sometimes called STIs or "sexually transmitted infections."

STDs such as HPV, pictured here, can only be **diagnosed** by a doctor using different tests.

STDs and STIs are **infectious** diseases that pass from one person to another, usually during sexual acts. There are many types of STDs, but they usually fall into one of three groups—bacteria, viruses, or **parasites**.

Some STDs have **symptoms**, such as pain, itching, and bumps. Others don't have symptoms. Those STDs are called asymptomatic.

There are several different types of STDs. Each has its own way of spreading and set of symptoms. The only certain way for you to know which one you have is to be tested by a doctor.

Common STDs in the United States (number of new cases/year):

- Human papillomavirus (HPV) (14.1 million)
- Chlamydia (2.86 million)
- Trichomoniasis (1.09 million)
- Gonorrhea (820,000)
- Herpes simplex virus type 2 (776,000)
- Syphilis (55400)
- Human immunodeficiency virus (HIV) (41400)

WHAT DEFINES SEX?

STDs usually are spread through sexual acts. But what exactly does that mean? You may realize there's more than just one way that people have sex. It's likely uncomfortable to talk about. But it's important to know because STDs can be spread through any of the following ways:

- Vaginal sex (penis-in-vagina sex)
- Oral sex (mouth-to-**genital** contact)
- Anal sex (penis-in-**anus** sex)
- Fingering or hand jobs (hand-to-genital contact)
- Dry humping or genital rubbing

You may think there's only one way to have sex, but there are many ways that STDs can be spread.

Chapter 2

HOW STDS SPREAD

STDs are spread from person to person through different ways. Some ways are sexual.

Infection often happens when people trade **bodily fluids**. This includes blood, vaginal fluids, and **semen**. The infection lives in these fluids.

Sharing a drinking glass with a friend can spread herpes.

When the infected fluids come into contact with an open wound on a healthy person, the infection can pass to them. It can also transmit to a second person when infected fluids touch the wet skin of the genitals or mouth. This skin is called a mucous membrane.

Mother to child during childbirth

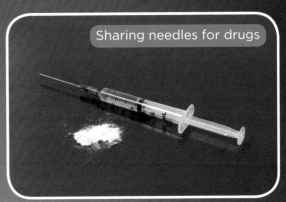
Sharing needles for drugs

STDs also can spread through nonsexual contact. This means the infections can pass from friend to friend, mother to child, and even stranger to stranger. It's not as common as sexual transmission, but it can still happen.

Nonsexual Ways to Get an STD

- Mother to child during childbirth
- Sharing towels or sheets
- Sharing razors
- Sharing needles for drugs
- Tattoos and piercings
- Kissing
- Unclean tanning beds
- Blood **transfusions**
- Breastfeeding
- Sharing drinks and food

Chapter 3

PREVENTING STDs

Preventing STDs is one of the most important things you can learn as you become an adult. If you use certain safety measures, you and your partners can stay healthy.

There are many tools you can use, like condoms and **vaccines**. But it's also important to talk to your partner. Talk about your sexual history and test results. Staying clearheaded is also key. People can make bad decisions when they're high or drunk. You don't want to forget to use a condom.

Dental dams are placed over the **vulva** or anus during oral sex.

WAYS TO PREVENT STDs

- **Abstinence:** Not having sex is the most effective way to prevent STDs.

- **Condoms:** Use one every time you have vaginal, anal, or oral sex.

- **Dental dams:** This piece of material protects you during oral sex.

- **Vaccines:** These can stop the spread of HPV and hepatitis B.

- **Testing:** Get regular screenings with a doctor.

- **Talk:** Tell your partner the results of STD tests.

- **Be safe:** Don't share needles, drinks, food, or towels.

HOW TO USE CONDOMS

A condom is a thin pouch worn on the penis. It blocks semen from entering the vagina, anus, or mouth. It also stops bodily fluids from entering the urethra of the penis, where urine comes out.

You can buy condoms at most grocery and drug stores. Many health clinics have them for free.

They're not foolproof, but correct use of condoms can improve their effectiveness.

Condoms come in a package all rolled up. To put one on, pinch the tip of the condom and place it at the head of the **erect** penis. Then unroll the condom down the penis.

SOME FACTS ABOUT CONDOMS

- They are not effective 100 percent of the time. They can break.

- Use a new condom each time you have sex.

- They don't protect against STDs that are spread through skin contact.

- There are female condoms that go in the vagina.

- Oil-based **lubricants** can cause them to break.

- If a condom breaks during sex, immediately stop.

Chapter 4

COMMON STDS

More than 110 million people in the United States have an STD. Many of them are young people aged 15 to 24. Here are some figures about STDs:

- Young people account for 50% of all new infections.
- 46% of high school students have had sex.
- New infections in teen girls (51%) are higher than teen boys (49%).
- 6 in 10 teens say they used condoms in most recent sexual acts.
- Black teens (19%) are more likely to have an STD than white teens (3%).

One in four teens gets an STD each year.

CHLAMYDIA

Chlamydia is one of the most common STDs in the United States. It's caused by harmful bacteria in men and women.

The infection is spread through bodily fluids during vaginal, anal, or oral sex. Using condoms can help prevent transmission. It can also pass from mother to baby during birth.

Chlamydia can spread to a woman's **uterus** and cause something called **pelvic** inflammatory disease (PID). PID can cause pain. It may make it hard for a woman to become pregnant later in life.

Some people might not have any symptoms at all from chlamydia.

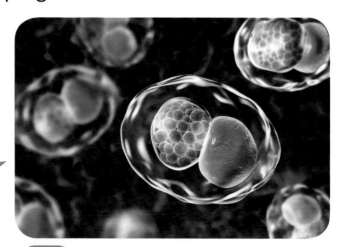

SYMPTOMS

- Burning while peeing
- Unusual **discharge** from penis, vagina, or anus
- Pain and swelling in testicles
- Pain or bleeding in anus
- Abdominal pain
- Painful sex for women
- Bleeding between periods for women
- Fever
- Eye infection in newborns

TESTING

- Pee samples
- Cotton swab to sample discharge

TREATMENT

- **Antibiotics**
- No sexual activity for seven days
- Get retested three months after treatment

PREVENTION

- Condoms
- Abstinence
- Get your partner tested and treated

Abdominal pain

HUMAN PAPILLOMAVIRUS

Human papillomavirus is best known as HPV. There are many types of HPV.

HPV is spread during vaginal, anal, or oral sex. It's the most common STD in the United States. More than 79 million people have it. Most people have no symptoms and don't know they have it.

Sometimes the virus goes away by itself. But sometimes it causes more problems. Men and women can get cancer on their genitals or even in their mouths.

There are more than 100 types of HPV. Fourteen of them can cause cancer.

SYMPTOMS

- Genital warts
- Unusual Pap smear (a vaginal test)
- If HPV has led to cervical cancer:
    - Bleeding between periods
    - Back, leg, or pelvic pain
    - Weight loss, tiredness, or loss of hunger
    - Swelling in legs

TESTING

- Pap smear
- Removal of cervical cells
- No test for men

PREVENTION

- Condoms
- Abstinence
- Vaccine

TREATMENT

- Medicine for genital warts

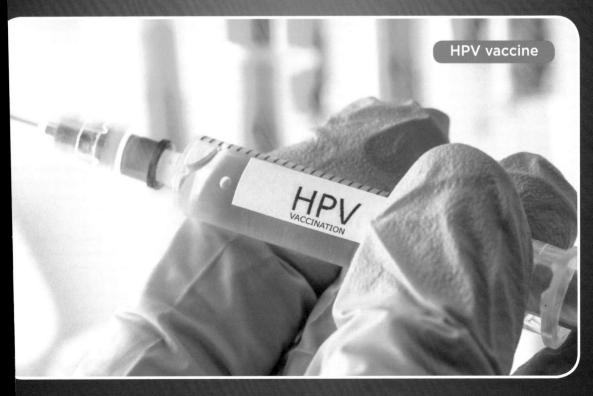

HPV vaccine

Getting Vaccinated

When I went for my yearly checkup this week, my doctor said I should get the HPV vaccine. At first, my mom and I said no. I'm only 15 years old. I'm not even sexually active!

My doctor said U.S. health officials say people should be vaccinated starting at age 11. The point is to be safe from the virus well before you're sexually active.

Mom and I decided I should go ahead and get the vaccine. That way I'll be prepared later in life. I got the vaccine during my visit but will have to come back again for two more shots.

The doctor said people younger than 15 should get two vaccines. People who are older need three.

HPV vaccines are mostly suggested for people ages 9 to 26.

TRICHOMONIASIS

Trichomoniasis is a sexually transmitted parasite. It's sometimes called trich. The disease usually is spread through bodily fluids during vaginal sex. It's rare for it to spread during oral or anal sex.

About 70 percent of people who have the parasite don't have symptoms. The most common symptom is irritation. It can easily be mistaken for other infections. The only way to be certain you have trich is to be tested.

Having it could make you more likely to get other STDs.

People who have trich but don't show any symptoms can still spread the STD.

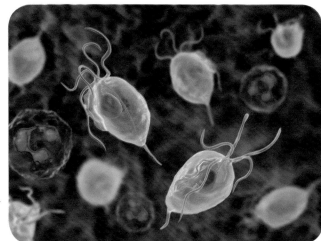

SYMPTOMS

- Irritation (itchy or painful genitals)
- Burning while peeing
- Discharge from penis
- Smelly discharge from vagina
- Pain during sex

TESTING

- Cotton swab to take sample of discharge

TREATMENT

- Antibiotics
- Partner tested and treated as well
- No sex until symptoms are gone and medicine is done

PREVENTION

- Condoms
- Abstinence
- Don't spread sexual fluids using hands
- Don't rub bare genitals with a partner

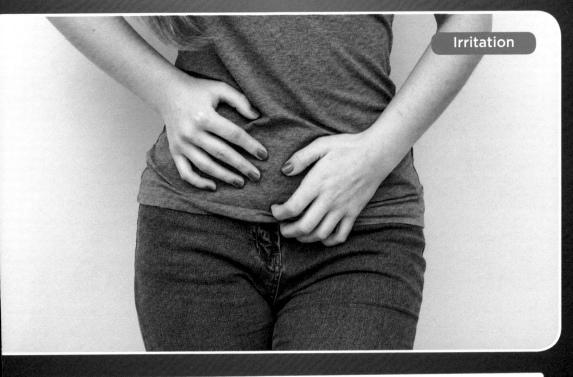

Irritation

GONORRHEA

Gonorrhea is a bacterial infection sometimes called the clap or the drip. Both men and women can have it, but men are more likely to show symptoms. It's spread through vaginal, anal, and oral sex. The disease can infect the genitals, anus, and even throat and eyes.

Like many other STDs, most people who have gonorrhea don't show symptoms. The only way to know for sure is to be tested.

With the right treatment, it can be **cured**. But if not cured, it can cause worse problems.

Untreated gonorrhea can spread to your blood, skin, heart, or joints. It can be deadly.

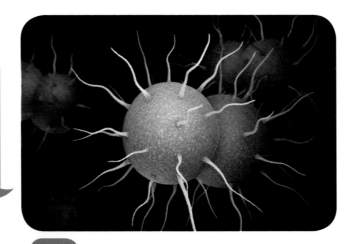

SYMPTOMS

- Burning while peeing
- Genital discharge
- Painful or swollen testicles
- Vaginal bleeding between periods
- Anal gonorrhea includes anal itching, bleeding, and discharge and pain when pooping

TESTING

- Urine sample
- Cotton swab to test throat, anus, or genital discharge

PREVENTION

- Condoms
- Abstinence

TREATMENT

- Antibiotics
- No sexual activity for seven days
- Retesting three months after treatment
- Partner tested and treated as well

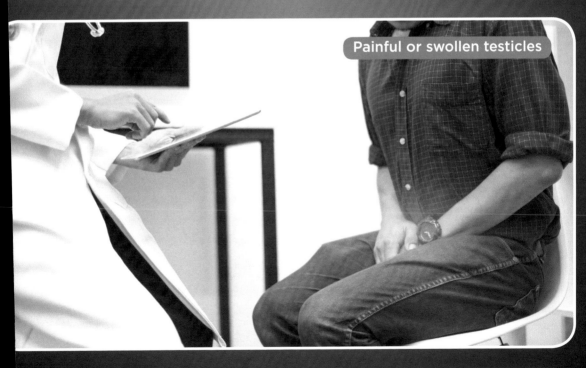

Painful or swollen testicles

GENITAL HERPES

Herpes simplex virus type 2 is one of many kinds of herpes. It's often called HSV-2 or genital herpes. It causes sores on the genitals. It's spread by skin-to-skin touch during vaginal, anal, or oral sex.

There's no cure for herpes. Once you get the virus, you will always have it. But sores aren't always present. When they are, it's called an outbreak.

HSV-2 is similar to another type of herpes called HSV-1. It causes cold sores on the mouth and genital sores after oral sex.

Genital herpes can be spread even when no sores are seen.

SYMPTOMS

- Sores on the genitals, anus, or mouth
- Fever and body aches during the first outbreak
- Itching
- Burning while peeing

TESTING

- Visual exam
- Collect fluid from sores
- Blood test

TREATMENT

- Antiherpes medicine to shorten outbreaks
- To ease pain:
  - Warm bath
  - Keep genital area dry
  - Wear loose clothing
  - Put ice packs on sores

PREVENTION

- Condoms
- Dental dams
- Avoid sex during outbreaks

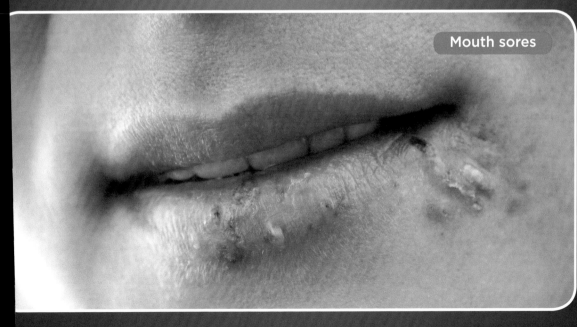

Mouth sores

SYPHILIS

Syphilis is a bacterial infection that can cause lots of harm to the body. It's spread by touching sores on the genitals, anus, or mouth. The disease has four stages based on how bad the symptoms are.

Mothers can pass syphilis on to their babies during childbirth.

If left untreated, it can spread to the brain or eyes, causing **paralysis**, mental illness, or blindness.

Doctors test for syphilis with a blood sample. They might also test fluid from a sore. It's curable with antibiotics.

Syphilis is prevented by using condoms or dental dams.

Primary Stage

- Lasts three to six weeks
- One or two sores

Secondary Stage

- Skin rash
- Sores
- Fever
- Sore throat
- Hair loss
- Headaches
- Weight loss
- Muscle aches
- Tiredness

Latent Stage

- Period when there are no symptoms

Tertiary Stage

- Begins about 10 to 30 years after start of infection
- Spreads to heart and blood
- Affects brain and **nervous system**
- Can cause death

HUMAN IMMUNODEFICIENCY VIRUS (HIV)

Human immunodeficiency virus, or HIV, is one of the best-known STDs. This is because of news attention it got in the 1980s when it was first seen.

HIV is spread through bodily fluids during vaginal, oral, and anal sex. There's no cure.

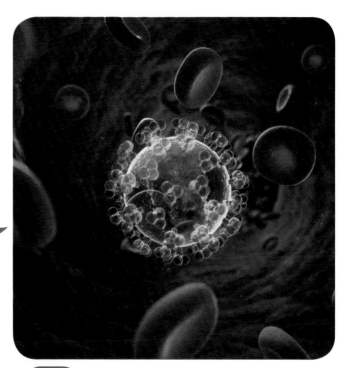

HIV weakens the immune system, which fights illness in the body. Left untreated, HIV can turn into acquired immunodeficiency syndrome, or AIDS. The symptoms of AIDS are even worse.

There have been great improvements in the treatment of HIV. This means there are fewer cases of AIDS in the United States now than in the 1980s.

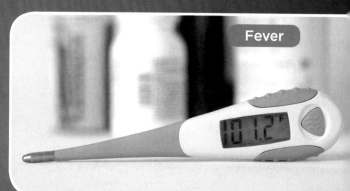
Fever

SYMPTOMS

- Sometimes don't show for years
- Fever and achiness
- Regular colds and other illnesses
- Bruising
- Shortness of breath
- Rashes
- Diarrhea
- Weight loss
- Headaches
- Dizziness
- Purplish spots on skin
- Bleeding from mouth, nose, anus, or vagina

TREATMENT

- Antiretroviral therapy medicine
- Eating well
- Getting enough sleep
- Exercise

TESTING

- Blood test
- Swab from inside your cheek

PREVENTION

- Condoms
- Dental dams
- PrEP medication

Living with HIV

My favorite uncle, Mark, has had HIV for about 10 years. He takes a bunch of medicine every day to help him stay healthy.

He told me last week that gay men like him are more likely to get the virus than others. Even though HIV sounds scary, doctors say he'll live into his 70s as long as he takes his medicine and treats his body well.

Uncle Mark says he feels lucky. A lot of his older friends in the gay community died young. In the 1980s and 1990s, people only lived up to 20 years with HIV. Sometimes less. It makes him very sad to think about.

New medicine, though, helps him live longer and makes him less likely to get AIDS.

HIV usually won't show up in tests the first few months after infection. People at risk should get tested often.

STIGMA

Many people worry about getting tested for STDs. Having such an infection can come with what's called stigma. This means people may have unfavorable feelings about a person because of their infection.

Anyone—gay or straight, male or female—can get any of the STDs this resource talks about.

This happened with HIV when the world first learned about it in the 1980s. Many people believed the only people to get HIV were those who were gay or used certain drugs. There was a lot of fear and misunderstanding.

Many STDs can be cured. Those that aren't curable are easy to treat.

AMERICANS WITH DISABILITIES ACT

There are laws to protect people with HIV and AIDS from being **discriminated** against. The Americans with Disabilities Act gives protection to people with disabilities—including those with HIV and AIDS.

This means your HIV status can't stop you from:

- Getting a job
- Working out at a gym
- Renting an apartment
- Hiring a moving company
- Getting dental treatment
- Attending a public school
- Going to overnight camp

Chapter 5

FINDING SUPPORT

If you or a friend think you might have an STD, there are many places you can turn for information. It can be a stressful time, but these resources can help.

Planned Parenthood

https://plannedparenthood.org

Call 1-800-230-PLAN to find a local clinic for (sometimes free) STD testing and free condoms.

Centers for Disease Control and Prevention

https://cdc.gov/std

Visit the website or call 1-800-232-4636 for info on STDs.

Crisis Text Line

https://crisistextline.org

Text HOME to 741741 for mental health help if you're feeling anxious or depressed.

Getting Tested

My best friend, Maria, called me up crying last week. I knew it must be bad because she only ever texts.

She said her ex-boyfriend told her he had tested positive for genital herpes. They've been broken up for several months, but his doctor said he might've passed the virus to Maria.

Maria was too scared to tell her mom. She also didn't have the money to pay for a doctor's visit.

Maria came over and we searched online. We found a clinic that does free testing one town over. I went with her to give her support.

Luckily, her test came back clear! We were so relieved. And while we were there, the nurses gave us each some free condoms.

In some states, teens are unable to get birth control without their parents' permission.

HAVING THE TALK

One of the most important tools in fighting STDs is talking to your partner. You should be open with each other even before you start thinking of having sex. If you test positive for an STD, you will need to tell your partner so that they can protect themselves. Your partner will also need to get tested.

It's better to have a talk about condom use before you start having sex. That way you're not making decisions while caught up in the moment.

It can be an uncomfortable topic to talk about, so it's good to plan ahead. Write down questions you might have. Make sure to be a good listener to your partner.

Before you begin having sex:

- Make plans to get STD tests together.
- Share if either of you have an STD.
- Make sure you both agree to use condoms and/or dental dams.
- Talk about getting an HPV vaccine if you haven't had it.
- Decide whether you want to use other forms of protection. Except abstinence, no one method is 100 percent safe.

The Next Step

Finding out I had chlamydia was really scary. But I was glad to finally know what was going on with my body! My doctor gave me a prescription for antibiotics and told me to stop having sex for a week. She also told me to come back for another test in a few months.

The hard part was when I had to tell my girlfriend. I made sure we had some time alone and I came clean to her. At first, she cried because she was worried she might be sick. She didn't have any symptoms.

I told her about the clinic I visited. We made plans for me to go with her to get tested.

> You can help stop STDs from spreading! Practice safe sex and be honest with your partner.

GLOSSARY

antibiotics: Medicine that stops infections.

anus: The opening in the buttocks where solid waste comes out.

bodily fluid: A liquid that comes from inside a person's body.

cure: To relieve a person of symptoms or a disease.

diagnosed: Having identified a disease by its signs and symptoms.

discharge: A substance that's released by the body.

discriminate: Unfair treatment based on factors, such as a person's race, age, religion, or gender.

erect: Rigidly upright or straight.

genitals: A person or animal's external organs for reproduction.

infectious: Producing or capable of producing infection, or sickness caused by germs entering the body.

lubricant: A liquid that reduces friction.

nervous system: The system of nerves that sends messages for controlling feeling and movement between the brain and body.

paralysis: The loss of the ability to move.

parasite: A living thing that lives in, on, or with another living thing and often harms it.

pelvic: Dealing with the pelvis, a bone and an area in the lower abdomen.

semen: The male reproductive fluid.

symptom: A sign that shows someone is sick.

transfusion: Transferring, or moving, donated blood into a person.

uterus: An organ in a woman's lower abdomen related to reproduction.

vaccines: Shots given to a person to keep them safe from an illness.

vulva: Female external genitals.

INDEX